EDUCATION AMONG THE JEWS

FROM THE EARLIEST TIMES TO THE END
OF THE TALMUDIC PERIOD, 500 A. D.

PAUL E. KRETZMANN, Ph. D.

WIPF & STOCK · Eugene, Oregon

Wipf and Stock Publishers
199 W 8th Ave, Suite 3
Eugene, OR 97401

Education Among the Jews
From the Earliest Times to the End of
theTalmudic Period, 500 A. D.
By Kretzmann, Paul E.
Softcover ISBN-13: 978-1-6667-6652-3
Hardcover ISBN-13: 978-1-6667-6653-0
eBook ISBN-13: 978-1-6667-6654-7
Publication date 12/2/2022
Previously published by The Talmud Society, 1922

This edition is a scanned facsimile of
 the original edition published in 1922.

INTRODUCTION

In publishing this little booklet, the author is very well aware that he is placing himself in the most unfavorable light and courting the most adverse and abject criticism of so-called scientific scholarship of the Bible. But he freely acknowledges and proudly confesses his absolute rejection of all scientific criticism of the Bible outside of textual research and stands squarely for the infallibility of Holy Scriptures. The Christ Whose words even the most rabid critics admit to be historically true: "The scripture cannot be broken," John 10,35. "Till heaven and earth pass, one jot or one tittle shall in no wise pass from the law, till all be fulfilled," Matth. 5,18., was either what He claimed to be, the eternal Son of God, Who gladly permitted the attribute of Omniscience to be ascribed to Him, and Who in these words is a frank exponent of the infallibility of Holy Scriptures, or He was the most despicable hypocrite and cheat the world has ever known. And I confess that I believe it far better to stand with Him foursquare against all criticism of His eternal word, which is the revelation of His divine Essence, than to stand on the uncertain ground of modern Biblical criticism and degenerate into a vapid spouter of moral platitudes. Much better by far to accept the inspired Scriptural account of the creation of the world and of the history of

the Jewish people word for word which has stood
the test of the ages and endured the vain mutterings
of foolish criticism both here and abroad than to accept the inane theory of a so-called cosmic evolu-
tion. Which is the more reasonable and more con-
formable with common sense: the plain, unadorned
Scriptural account that bears on its face the stamp of
veracity, or the bolstered-up bombast of the forfend-
ers of evolutionistic doctrines? The author's stand
will not be misconstrued by people that have made
a study of both sides of the question. In any question pertaining to this world's wisdom I believe in
research and criticism to the full extent, but far be
it from me to profane the Holy Book of God with
sacrilegious hands. So much for the spirit in which
the author has used the Bible as source material.

So far as the *subject matter* is concerned, the
word education is here used in its widest sense, including the entire bringing-up of the children, at
home as well as in the school. Only in this way
may justice be done to the people whose educational
history is here briefly outlined.

The *form* may seem clumsy to the casual reader,
but it will certainly aid in reference work, since the
periods treated are those of Hasting's Bible Dictionary.

The author freely acknowledges his indebtedness
to the Rev. Prof. W. H. T. Dau, of St. Louis, Mo.,
for looking over the manuscript.

St. Paul, Minn., June, 1915.

CONTENTS

CONTENTS

Education Among the Jews

I

THE NATIVE PERIOD

From the Earliest Times to the Division of the Kingdom, 953 B. C.

(a) *Before the Flood*

THE history of the Jewish people, if we may speak of them as such at this time of the world, is told briefly in the first six chapters of Genesis. In this age of the infancy of the world, there is no record of any special transmittance of knowledge, of any system of education. That the history of the first people was handed down, by tradition, from father to son, is, of course, very evident from the preserved narrative. And that the moral precepts and the Gospel news of salvation were transmitted in much the same manner, appears from Gen. 4,26: "Men began to proclaim the name of the Lord." That the traditions were discussed quite freely and were made a basis of fervent hope, is shown in the case of Eve,

Gen. 4,1; "I have gained (by creative bearing) a man—the Lord," and that of Lamech, who said, after the birth of Noah: "This same shall comfort us concerning our work and toil of our hands, because of the ground which the Lord hath cursed," Gen. 5, 29. Both of these expressions have the same motive, the hope in the coming Messiah, the seed of the woman. Whether the various kinds of handicraft and arts, which had their inception in these early days, such as the music of Jubal and the brass-and ironwork of Tubalcain, were transmitted by any method but that of teaching the craft to the sons, is not apparent, although Jubal is called the father of all such as handle the harp and organ, Gen. 4, 21. Whether Lamech, on account of his poetical couplets, Gen. 4, 23, 24, is to be regarded as the father of poetry, is a question which has often been discussed. Owing to the meagre source material, definite conclusions can hardly be drawn.

(b) The Patriarchal Period

After the flood and the subsequent confusion of tongues, the real history of the Jewish people opens with the journey of Abram, afterwards Abraham, from Mesopotamia to the Land of Promise. His sojourn there was marked by various incidents, chief of which was the birth of Isaac. The blessing of Abraham was transmitted by Isaac to Jacob, the second son of Rebecca, who thereupon had to flee to Mesopotamia. The sons of Jacob became the forefathers of the twelve tribes of Israel. Joseph, one of these sons, became the savior of his brothers during the great famine and obtained for them and their children a place of refuge in the land of Goshen. For several centuries the children of Israel lived in Egypt, until, with a change in the reigning dynasty, there came a crisis in the affairs of the people. Moses became the leader of his brethren, led them out of the house of bondage and to the very borders of Palestine.

(c) *The Time of the Judges*

Joshua took the place of Moses at the boundary of the new country. Under his leadership the tribes which inhabited the land were subjugated and the country divided among the twelve tribes of Israel, Judah and Benjamin occupying the southern part, Reuben, Gad, and Manasseh principally the land east of the Jordan, and Asher, Dan, Ephraim, Issachar, Naphtali, Simeon, and Zebulun, the northern and eastern part. The form of government at this time was theocratic, the people being guided entirely by the laws and ordinances which Moses had delivered to them. Although the tribes had received the command to annihilate the heathen nations, some of these had been spared. And these were the very ones that made constant inroads upon the country, harassing the inhabitants and plundering and robbing their property. At such times Judges (Saviors) were called to lead the people against the enemy. This entire period was a time of unrest, of an attempt to accommodate themselves to new conditions The unfortunate ones that had been held in the serfdom of Egypt, had all died in the wilderness; their children occupied the Land of Promise, they were obliged to become accustomed both to liberty and to self-government, or rather self-restraint. Under such conditions a well-ordered community can hardly be conceived of.

(d) *The Time of David and Solomon*

With the growing prosperity of the people and the feeling of national power there came the demand for a king, as all the heathen about them had. Samuel, who at that time was the spiritual leader of the people, was very angry with them for the request they voiced. But his objections were overruled and Saul was chosen by lot as the first king of the Jewish nation. The beginning of his reign was very successful, but after a few years he turned aside from the divine ways. This apostasy, together with the wars

against the heathen nations and the persecutions of
David, made the last years of his reign more of a
curse than a blessing for Israel and hindered the development of the nation perceptibly. The reign of
David, second king of Israel, opened rather unfav-
orably with a revolt of a faction of Saul and wars
against the Jebusites and other heathen nations. The
successful termination of all these difficulties gave
David a position of power and gained for his people
an era of prosperity and peace. Moreover, since
David himself was a poet and writer of the foremost
rank, he very greatly favored the arts and sciences.
This happy state of affairs continued and became
even more pronounced during the reign of Solomon,
the "wise" king. His accession marked the beginning of the first "golden era" of the Jewish people.
This happy state was not to endure for a long time
though. Rehoboam, the son of Solomon, began his
reign with a foolish decision. The result was that
ten of the tribes seceded and formed a kingdom of
their own, while only two, Judah and Benjamin, remained with Rehoboam.

Education During the Native Period

As stated above, the history of the Jewish people
really begins with the coming of Abraham to the
Promised Land. Abraham was therefore at all

times looked upon as the father of the Jews, or Hebrews, as they were called very early, perhaps in al-
lusion to their coming across the river Jordan. And
the very history of Abraham furnishes evidence for
the early germs of education in the Jewish people.
If Abraham had not been a prince of royal blood or
a member of the nobility in his native country, Chaldea, he at least had been a member of a prominent
and wealthy family. He also associated on terms
of equality with the king of Egypt, with Melchize-
dek, the king of Salem, and with Abimelech, the
king of Gerar. He was therefore at different times
of his life in close contact with the Chaldean, with
the Egyptian, and with the Hittite learning. Now
the civilization of Babylonia (Mesopotamia and
Chaldea) was at that time very far advanced. Reading and writing were general attainments throughout
the country. According to Prof. Sayce, schools and
libraries were flourishing in Babylonia long before
Abraham was born, and the arts and sciences were
fostered. The Babylonia of the age of Abraham
was a more highly educated country than the Eng-
land of George III. The same was true of Egypt.
The country was full of schools and libraries, of
teachers and pupils, of poets and prose writers, and
of literary works which they had composed. The
man of business, the wealthier fellaheen, even to
overseers of the workmen, were acquainted with

the hieroglyphic system of writing and the hieratic or
cursive hand which had developed out of it. No one
could live in Egypt without coming under the spell
of its literary culture. As to the Hittites finally,
whose very existence was denied a few years ago, re-
cent explorations and excavations have proved definitely that this people also possessed a high degree
of learning and exerted a more or less pronounced
influence on some of the nations with whom they
came in contact. The possibility of Abraham's having remained uninfluenced by the culture with which
he was in almost continual contact, can hardly be
conceived of. Josephus even goes so far as to say:
"He (Abraham) communicated to them (the Egyptians) arithmetic and delivered to them the science
of astronomy; for, before Abram came into Egypt,
they were unacquainted with those parts of learning"
(Antiq. of the Jews, Book I, Ch. VIII, 2). The
Jewish people then present the somewhat unique example of having as their progenitor a wealthy, influential, and highly cultured man, whose influence
along educational lines was bound to be most marked.

The following patriarchs, Isaac and Jacob, occupied a position which was hardly less prominent.
Neither were their relations with the heathen nations less significant or without permanent influence.
And while it may readily be admitted that the no-
madic life of the sons of Jacob as well as the sojourn

in Egypt were not conducive to literary and artis-
tic advancement, it must be remembered, on the other hand, that both Joseph and Moses received, the
former a part, the latter all of his training, at Helio-
polis, the college city of Egypt. Of Moses especially it was said that he was learned in all the wisdom of the Egyptians, and was mighty in words and
in deeds, Acts 7, 22. It is also hardly conceivable
that a contact with the learning of Egypt, which
lasted for several centuries, should not have left its
impression on the young nation in its own country.
During the centuries when the Jews were without a
stable government, the efforts to establish and maintain an educational system may indeed have been
more or less desultory, but the strength of the hier-
archical system as well as the principle of the theo-
cracy, at least outwardly upheld, may be cited as an
argument in favor of at least a partial educational
system as well as one against general education.
Jewish tradition has it that there were regular established schools as early as the time of Isaac, and
that Jacob and Esau both attended the primary
school. We have no way of either substantiating or
disproving tradition on this score. Skeptics may dis-
claim the very possibility of so great an achieve-
ment at so early a date. But it will always be well
to remember that an argument "e silentio" has very
little in its favor, while the fact that the patriarchs

had a household embracing several hundred souls
and could very well enjoy the services of stewards,
would surely not preclude the possibility of their em-
ploying a teacher for their clan. And if so much
may be said in favor of a well-developed educational
system at so early a date, the assumption of at least
a rudimentary stage in education at the time of the
Judges can hardly be said to be too daring. The
factors favoring a more thorough establishment of
an educational system with the beginning of the
Monarchial Period have been outlined above. Everything that is related of David and Solomon makes
the probability of their having been the patrons of
the arts and sciences more certain. The "golden era"
was one of peace, not war.

After this preliminary general survey we are now
prepared to understand the specific instances of educational references in the historical books of the
Jews pertaining to this time.

The very *high regard* in which the Jews held
children as gifts of God and their earnest and pray-
erful longing for offspring colored and influenced
their whole life. Eve's joyous cry at the birth of
Cain: "I have gotten a man from the Lord," Gen.
4, 1, is usually cited as an instance of the longing of
the people of the old covenant for the promised
Messiah. But aside from this evident interpretation
there is an underlying thought which voices the sen-

timent of the mothers of the old covenant. The verb *kanah* is used principally of supernatural, creative begetting, so that Eve's thought also included: The Lord has graciously granted to me, through special creative power, a son. It is said of Jacob Gen. 37, 3: "Now Israel loved Joseph more than all his children, because he was the son of his old age." The fervent longing and earnest supplication of Hannah, the wife of Elkanah, is voiced in the prayer 1 Sam. 1, 11: "Give unto thine handmaid a manchild." So highly did Hannah, together with the other women of Israel, value the gift of children, that her barrenness rested upon her as a curse of God. So sincere was her longing for a son that she promised in a vow that she would give back her son to the Lord, i. e. that she would have him trained for divine service from his infancy. And she fully redeemed her vow when she brought the young Samuel to the priest Eli at the tabernacle, when the boy was but three years old. Other instances illustrating the same love and longing for children are the examples of Sarah, Gen. 16, 1, 2, Rebeccah, Gen. 25, 21, Rachel, Gen. 30, 1, Ruth, Ruth 4, 13, and Michal, 2 Sam. 6, 23.

But not only in these specific instances is the high regard and the tender love of parents toward their children set forth, but also in passages of a general nature, thus proving conclusively that the Jews made this a basic principle in their national life. A poem of the time of Solomon contains the well-known lines: "Lo, children are an heritage of the Lord, and the fruit of the womb is his reward. As arrows in the hands of a mighty man, so are children of the youth. Happy is the man that has his quiver full of them!" Ps. 127, 3-5. And again: "Thy wife shall be as a fruitful vine by the sides of thy house, thy children like olive plants round about thy table. Behold that thus shall be blessed the man that feareth the Lord. . . . Yea, thou shalt see thy children's children, and peace upon Israel!" Ps. 128, 3, 4, 6. The same sentiment is voiced Prov. 3, 12b, where a father is spoken of as delighting in his son. The verb *razah* used here means 'to love, to be well pleased with.' It is represented as a paternal trait of character, as a foregone conclusion that a parent love his son and take delight and pride in him.

In thorough accordance with this position of the parents we find the *attitude* of the *children toward their parents* and toward all those in authority. When, after the incident at Shechem, Jacob reproved his sons, they accepted the rebuke, thus recognizing their father's authority, Gen. 34, 30. The motive that prompted Joseph to bring the evil report of his brothers before the father, was doubtless principally one of loyalty to authority, Gen. 37, 2. When all the sons and daughters rose up to comfort Jacob, there was as much recognition of his position as remorse for their evil deed in their action, Gen. 37, 30. When the Jews received the Law by the hands of Moses, they were not left in doubt as to the authority which God had given the parents. The commandment of the Decalogue reads: "Honor thy father and thy mother, that thy days may be long upon the land which the Lord thy God giveth thee," Ex. 20, 12. This is emphasized Lev. 19, 3: "Ye shall fear every man his mother and his father," and repeated Deut. 5, 16: "Honor thy father and thy mother, as the Lord thy God hath commanded thee." In conformity with these commandments we read: "My son, keep thy father's commandments, and forsake not the law of thy mother: Bind them continually upon thy heart, and tie them about thy neck. When thou goest it shall lead thee; when thou sleepest, it shall keep thee, and when thou awakest, it shall talk with thee," Prov. 6, 20-22. In the same way: "Hearken unto thy father that begat thee, and despise not thy mother when she is old," Prov. 23, 22. That the authority of the parents was sovereign, is evident from Prov. 19, 26: "He that wasteth (shows lack of respect toward, is contemptuous toward) his father and chaseth away his mother, is a son that causeth shame, and bringeth reproach." And again Prov. 28, 24: "Whoso robbeth his father and his mother and saith: It is no transgression, the same is the companion of a detroyer."

These principles necessitated the maintenance of the strictest and most uncompromising *discipline.* The first step in discipline was *earnest admonition, reprimand,* and *reproof.* Prov. 1, 8: "My son, hear the instruction (Hebr. *musar,* admonition) of thy father, and forsake not the law of thy mother." Prov. 13, 1: "A wise son heareth his father's instruction; but a scorner heareth not rebuke (German: Der Spoetter hoert nicht auf Verweise)." Prov. 15, 5: "A fool despiseth his father's instruction; but he that regardeth reproof is prudent." Prov. 3, 12: "Whom the Lord loveth He correcteth" (*jakah,* Greek *paideuo*). Prov. 6, 23b: "Reproofs of instruction are the way of life" (rebuking reprimands, Greek: *kai elegchos kai paideia;* French: *les remonstrances de la discipline*).

If reprimands and remonstrances proved futile, the next step in discipline was *corporal punishment,* usually in the form of *whipping.* Prov. 13, 24: "He that spareth his rod hateth his son, but he that loveth him chasteneth him betimes." Such punishing should, however, be done without carnal anger and in moderation. Prov. 19, 18: "Chasten thy son why there is hope, and let not thy soul spare for his crying" (Hebr.: but to kill him let not thy soul be driven). Prov. 22, 15: "Foolishness is bound in the heart of a child, but the rod of correction shall drive it far from him." Prov. 23, 13, 14: "Withhold not correction from the child: for if thou beatest him with a rod, he shall not die. Thou shalt beat him with a rod and shalt deliver his soul from hell." Prov. 29, 15, 17: "The rod and reproof give wisdom, but a child left to himself bringeth his mother to shame. Correct (punish) thy son, and he shall give thee rest, yea, he shall give delight unto thy soul." It was an exceedingly wise provision that punishment of this kind was to be tempered with wisdom and moderation, having in mind always the end to be gained, the welfare of the child and of the whole community, rather than a base desire for vengeance or the venting of a spite.

When even the harsher methods failed, then the final step was *expulsion* and *exile,* and even *death*. The latter punishment, however, was in the hands of the community or government, the parents themselves having no jurisdiction over life and death. In the case of the unruly Ishmael in the house of Abraham, Sarah's request was brief and to the point: "Cast out this bondwoman and her son, for the son of this bondwoman shall not be heir with my son," Gen. 21, 10. Deut. 27, 16: "Cursed be he that setteth light by his father or mother," Prov. 20, 20: "Whoso curseth his father or his mother, his lamp shall be put out in obscure darkness." It is not evident from the text whether a general curse is here pronounced, or whether the specific punishment is exile or death. That the final, most severe punishment was by no means beyond the pale of possibility, appears from several passages, for which no claim of ambiguity may be advanced. Prov. 30, 17: "The eye that mocketh at his father, and despiseth to obey his mother, the ravens of the valley shall put it out, and the young eagles shall eat it." The instances, in which capital punishment was prescribed by God, are carefully enumerated. Ex. 21, 15, 17: "He that smiteth his father or his mother, shall be surely put to death. He that curseth his father or his mother, shall surely be put to death." Lev. 20, 9: "For every one that curseth his father or his mother, shall be surely put to death; he hath cursed his father or his mother: his blood shall be upon him." In Deut. 21, 18-21, the entire mode of procedure in a case of this kind is outlined. A stubborn and rebellious son was to be brought to the elders of the city in the gate, where the formal accusation and condemnation should be made, "and all the men of his city shall stone him with stones, that he die: so shalt thou put evil away from among you, and all Israel shall hear, and fear."

With such strict discipline it was inevitable that good results were obtained, at least in outward drill, in training by rote. *Instruction in the fundamentals of the Law* or moral training was the basis of education. Prov. 1, 1-6 speaks in general of instruction in wisdom, justice, judgment, and equity. So far as moral efficiency and breadth of view is concerned, this would make an excellent basis for Milton's requirement. Prov. 2, 10, 11: "When wisdom entereth into thine heart, and knowledge is pleasant unto thy soul; discretion shall preserve thee, understanding shall keep thee." Prov. 4, 5: "Get wisdom, get understanding, forget it not." Prov. 16, 16: "How much better it is to get wisdom than gold! and to get understanding rather to be chosen than silver." These texts are so general that it hardly seems possible to limit them to a knowledge of the Law alone, although indeed Ps. 111, 10, says: "The fear of the Lord is the beginning of wisdom, a good understanding have all they that do his commandments." And Job 28, 28: "Unto man he said: Behold the fear of the Lord, that is wisdom, and to depart from evil is understanding." Religious teaching and moral training were the basis, the very foundation of education among the Jews in this period. The precepts of the books of this period have set the standard of morality for the whole world. The virtues that were emphasized and lauded in these books have received the approval of the ages, and the vices there condemned are considered so universally to this day. The praise of an ideal housewife Prov. 31, 10-31 is called the golden ABC of the wedded woman and regarded as the best presentation of so comprehensive a subject that has ever appeared.

But while the ancient Jews thus made religious training the basic principle of their education, they did not neglect *secular teaching*. The art of *writing* and therefore also of *reading* was undoubtedly known to Abraham, as shown above, and there are evidences throughout this period that it was a very general accomplishment. Joseph in Egypt (Gen. 41, 49) surely made use of it. Moses wrote the words of the Law at the command of God, Ex. 17, 14. Ex. 24, 4. Deut. 31, 9, 22. So general was this attainment that the command was given to all Israelites: "Thou shalt write them (the words of the Law) upon the door-posts of thy house, and upon thy gates," Deut. 11, 20. Moses also commanded the people to set up great stones, when they had come into the Promised Land, "and thou shalt write upon them all the words of this law, when thou art passed over," Deut. 27, 2, 3. The passage Joshua 4 does not in any way conflict with this statement, because the stones spoken of there were merely monuments. The men whom Joshua sent out described the land in a book, Josh. 18, 9. Joshua himself wrote, Josh. 24, 26. Samuel wrote, 1 Sam. 10, 25. The Book of Jasher was written, 2 Sam. 1, 18.

David wrote a letter, 2 Sam. 11, 14-16. That there were special scribes or secretaries at that time (2 Sam. 8, 17) does not signify any more than it does at the present time. See also Judges 8, 14.

Where writing and reading were such general accomplishments it is hardly conceivable that other branches of learning should have been neglected entirely. From the exactness of descriptions in Exodus, Deuteronomy, and Joshua, there must have been some knowledge of *geography* during this period. There was also at least some knowledge of *arithmetic,* if not of *geometry,* most likely also of *astronomy* (Job), and of *music* (1 Chron. 16, 42. 1 Chron. 25).

The training in this period, at least in the earlier part, so far as is apparent from Biblical sources, was in the hands of the *parents*, although it is by no means improbable that there were special teachers or tutors at a very early time. Perhaps it was held merely that the parents had to assume all responsibility for the training of their children. Gen. 18, 19, it is said of Abraham: "I know he will command his children and his household after him, and they shall keep the way of the Lord, to do justice and judgment." Deut. 6, 6, 7: "And these words which I command thee this day, shall be in thine heart: and thou shalt teach them diligently unto thy children" (drill thy children in them). Deut. 11, 18-

20: "Therefore shall ye lay up these my words in your heart and in your soul . . . and ye shall teach them your children, speaking of them when thou sittest in thine house, and when thou walkest by the way, when thou liest down, and when thou risest up." Ex. 10, 2: "That thou mayest tell in the ears of thy son, and of thy son's son, what things I have wrought in Egypt." Ps. 71, 18: "O God forsake me not, until I have shewed thy strength unto this generation, and thy power to every one that is to come." Ps. 78, 3, 4. "I will utter dark sayings of old which we have heard and known, and our fathers have told us. We will not hide them from their children, shewing to the generations to come the praises of the Lord and his strength. Vs. 6. That the generations to come might know them, even the children which should be born; who should arise and declare them to their children." Prov. 22, 6: "Train up a child in the way he should go; and when he is old, he will not depart from it." This passage has often been misconstrued, the contention being that the text speaks of unfolding or developing natural gifts and abilities. But an examination of the Hebrew text shows the verb *chanak*, which can be understood of initiatory rites only. Besides, the passage is evident-.ly objective. The German translation: Wie man einen Knaben gewoehnt; and the French: Instruis le jeune enfant à l'entrée de sa voie; are truer to the original.

Outside of the home, education was to some extent in the hands of the *priests*. Samuel was educated by Eli, the priest at Shiloh, 1 Sam. 2, 11, 21. The Jewish tradition that Samuel established *prophet schools* at Ramah and elsewhere, seems to be borne out by 1 Sam. 10, 10, and 1 Sam. 19, 19. So far as *private teachers* or *tutors* are concerned, Nathan seems to have occupied that position in the house of David, 2 Sam. 12, 25.

But there were also *professional teachers,* whether apart from the hierarchy or not, cannot be determined definitely. They were known as 'teachers' or 'men of wisdom.' Ps. 84, 7: "The teachers are blessed abundantly." Ps. 119, 99, 100: "I have more understanding than all my teachers." Ps. 141, 6: "When their judges (wise men) are overthrown in stony places." Prov. 5, 13: "Have not obeyed the voice of my teachers." Prov. 13, 20: "He that walketh with wise men shall be wise."

There is no evidence pointing to the existence of special rooms or buildings for school purposes, although this idea would not be excluded. The instruction that was not given at home or in the dwelling of the teacher, may well have been imparted in the conversational form, as indicated in some of the passages above, of which we have a striking example in the methods of Jesus at a later period. The school for musicians mentioned above was in Jerusalem, since its purpose was to train singers and musicians for chorus and orchestra work in connection with the liturgical part of the temple services.

II

THE PROPHETIC PERIOD, 953-586 B. C.

Historical Survey

WITH the division of the kingdom under Rehoboam there began a gradual disintegration of the nation. The northern kingdom of Israel, owing perhaps to a lack of vitality and stamina, was the first to suffer. Its rulers were, for the most part, conscienceless, immoral, selfish creatures, overbearing, cruel, and rapacious, so far as their own subjects were concerned, and fawning and hypocritical toward the mightier rulers of the surrounding countries. Jeroboam, the leader of the secessionist forces, was the first king of Israel. He was followed, in turn, by Nadab, Baesa, Ela, Simri, and Amri. Under Ahab the country suffered from a severe and prolonged drought. His introduction of Phoenician worship was a prime factor in overthrowing tradition and ancient usages. Even the schools of the prophets, which were by this time an established institution, did not escape his tyrannical policy, 1 Kings 18, 22. The country, torn by internal dissensions, had no strength to combat an aggressive adversary. It was only by marshalling all his forces that Ahab succeeded in defeating the Syrian king, Ben-Hadad. There followed several weak rulers, Ahaziah and Jehoram. Jehu had a long, but not exceptionally successful reign. It is significant that the final ruin of the nation began at this time: "In those days the Lord began to cut Israel short," 2 Kings 10, 32. Jehoahaz and Jehoash had a rather colorless reign. Under Jeroboam II Israel once more, by a last effort, regained a position of respect and power. He extended the boundaries of his kingdom to the Euphrates in the East, to Damascus in the North, to the Dead Sea in the South. His son, Zachariah, however, ruled only six months. His assassin Shallum was in turn slain by Menahem. It was only by the payment of high tribute that this ruler was able to maintain a semblance of a kingdom over against the Assyrians. His son, Pekahiah was murdered after a short reign by Pekah. After this ruler had, in turn, been removed by assassination, Hoshea, the murderer, became guilty of a last foolish move. He refused to pay tribute to the Assyrian king Shalmaneser, trying, at the same time, to win So, the king of Egypt, with presents. So the end came rather abruptly. Hoshea, together with the people of Israel, was led away into Assyrian captivity. And the result is stated thus: "Therefore the Lord removed them out of his sight: there was none left but the tribe of Judah only," 2 Kings 17, 18.

The history of the kingdom of Judah is not quite so dark and cheerless, but is also nothing but a recital of gradual disintegration and final ruin. Even under Rehoboam, the kingdom became so weak that, for the first time, an enemy succeeded in taking the city of Jerusalem. That was Shishak, king of Egypt. He even dared to plunder the temple and the palace which Solomon had built. Under the reign of Abijah and Asa things began to look better. Some of the strongest enemies were conquered or gained for Judah, and when the reformation of the Church and the judiciary was completed under Jehoshaphat, an era of renewed prosperity began for the southern kingdom. This did not last very long, however, With Jehoram, a gradual decline set in, which was intensified under the following rulers: Ahaziah, the queen-regent Athaliah, Joash, and Amaziah. The accession of Uzziah ushered in a century of greater prosperity. He was very fortunate in war and took a great deal of interest in the welfare of his people. These favorable conditions continued under Jotham, were reversed very markedly under Ahaz, but were emphasized under Hezekiah, the last king of importance. He made every effort to restore Judah to the glory of its "golden era." But it was the last flickering before the final extinction. The fate of the northern kingdom, which was settled during his reign, presaged the fate of Judah. The remaining kings Manasseh, Amon, Josiah, Jehoahaz, Jehoiakim, Jehoiachin, Zedekiah, were, almost to a man, either violently deposed or assassinated. In the year 605 B. C. Nebuchadnezzar took the first captives to Babylon, and twenty years later the remaining Jews with the exception of a little band which fled to Egypt, taking the unwilling Jeremiah with them, were led away into the Babylonian captivity.

Education during the Prophetic Period

It is evident from this brief historical survey that the conditions in both kingdoms were decidedly unfavorable to education and the fostering of the arts and sciences in general. For under such conditions of uncertainty and internal strife, of turmoil, disruption, and disintegration, the highest development of a people in sciences and arts cannot be reached, or if it has been attained to before, it cannot be maintained, or, at least, its existence is an extremely precarious one. The country was torn by civil war, overrun by hostile forces, the very existence of the nation was often threatened, and its final ruin but a question of time.

But while there are evidences of retrogression in certain respects, while there were times when systematic education for the masses was out of the question, it is significant that the *educational ideals of the people were not altered*. We have essentially the same precepts, the same means, and the same aims as in the previous period. And whenever there was an interval of peace, the recovery of lost ground was little short of marvellous.

So far as the *attitude of parents* toward their children is concerned, there is the same longing for offspring, the same love of children, the same authority over the young, as in the early days of Jewish history. The Shunammite at the time of Elisha had one supreme wish, that of becoming a mother to a son, 2 Kings 4, 16. And when her desire had been fulfilled and her boy afterward died, her great love for the child is shown in her every word and action, 2 Kings 4, 28. As one of the greatest curses of God pronounced upon a disobedient people, is mentioned "the miscarrying womb, and dry breasts," Hosea 9, 14. That the authority of parents over their children was in no wise curtailed, is evident from the passage Jer. 29, 6: "Take wives for your sons, and give your daughters to husbands." The example of Tobith is sufficient to show that this authority was unquestioned. That there were times, however, when the respect of the children toward their parents was forgotten, and the honor due to their station was not accorded them, appears from

Micah 7, 6: "The son dishonoreth the father, the daughter riseth up against her mother, the daughter-in-law against her mother-in-law." But of course the very fact that such a complaint was voiced is sufficient evidence for the assumption that the position of the parents as the natural superiors of the children was rigidly upheld and guarded.

This is evident also from the methods of *discipline* which were employed. The rigor of the previous period had in no wise been mitigated. Is. 45, 10: "Woe unto him that saith unto his father, What begettest thou? or to the woman, What hast thou brought forth?" This 'woe' of which the text speaks is undoubtedly the same punishment which is spoken of in the Law, and consisted in either expulsion or death.

Upon the parents rested the responsibility for the education of the children, especially their *moral* and *religious training*. As the Law had been passed on from father to son throughout the generations, and had been preserved also through the agency of the prophets and priests and other teachers, so the prophecies should be preserved by tradition. "Tell ye your children of it, and let your children tell their children, and their children another generation," Joel 1, 3. The worship of Jahweh indeed often gave way to the worship of Baal, at least by a part of the people, and religious training in the specific Jewish religion was often virtually abandoned, as in the days of Elijah, but occasional efforts at reformation, as those of Jehoshaphat, Uzziah, and Hezekiah, served to keep interest in the Jewish religion awake. Whenever such eras were ushered in, there was a revival of old-time religious instruction. To this, no doubt, Joel had reference, when he writes: "Be glad then, ye children of Zion, and rejoice in the Lord your God, who giveth you teachers unto righteousness," Joel 2, 23. That the *prophet schools* were continued, at least in the early part of this period, is evident from several passages. "The sons of the prophets came forth to Elisha," 2 Kgs. 2, 3, 5. "Fifty men of the sons of the prophets went and stood to view afar off," vs. 7, 15. "And Elisha came again to Gilgal: and there was a dearth in the land: and the sons of the prophets were sitting before him," 2 Kings 4, 38 ff. There were, according to the text, one hundred men at this school. "And the sons of the prophets said unto Elisha, Behold now, the place where we dwell with thee is too strait for us. Let us go, we pray thee, unto Jordan, and take thence every man a beam, and let us make a place there, where we may dwell," 2 Kings 6, 1 ff. It appears from these passages that the prophet schools at this time were boarding schools, the buildings of which were erected by the pupils themselves, and who were supported, to a great extent, by voluntary contributions and loans. "There came a man from Baalshalisha, and brought the man of God bread of the first fruits, twenty loaves of barley, and full ears of corn in the husk thereof. And he said, Give unto the people that they may eat. And his servitor said, What? should I set this before an hundred men?" 2 Kings 4, 42, 43. It is not expressly stated whether there was any instruction outside of the teaching of the Law, but from the entire history of the time it would surely not be too bold to conclude that reading and writing were also taught. In fact, in carrying out the commands of the Torah, it devolved upon the leaders of the prophet schools to teach their pupils to read and to write.

In many of the royal houses of this period we find private *tutors,* to whom the education of the children was entrusted. In the case of Ahab's children these men are called 'bringers-up of the children,' 2 Kings 10, 1, 5. Jehoiada, the priest, was tutor and guardian of king Joash, 2 Chron. 24. Uzziah had Zechariah for a teacher at his court, 2 Chron. 26, 5. It is very probable that the training which the royal children of the Jewish nation received was quite as far advanced as that of the princes in the surrounding countries.

However, there was also instruction for the people in general, with specially trained *teachers*. Jehoshaphat "in the third year of his reign sent to his princess . . . to teach in the cities of Judah. and with them he sent Levites . . . and priests. And they taught in Judah, and had the book of the law of the Lord with them, and went about throughout all the cities of Judah, and taught the people," 2 Chron. 17, 7-9. The scribe (*sofer*), the learned man, seems to have been the professional teacher from this time on. "Where is the scribe?" Is. 33, 18. "Thy teachers (interpreters) have transgressed against me," Is. 43, 27. "The Lord God hath given me the tongue of the learned" (professional teacher), Is. 50, 4. "The priests said not, Where is the Lord and they that handle the law knew me not: the pastors also transgressed against me, and the prophets prophecied by Baal," Jer. 2, 8. Although the argument of variation might be advanced here, the fact that the words were in use seems to point to the existence of separate offices. "From the prophet even unto the priest every one dealeth falsely," Jer. 6, 13. "The law shall perish from the priest, and counsel from the ancients," Hesek. 7, 26. This is commonly regarded to mean that there were teachers outside of the priests, who were interpreters of the Law, expounding it in the schools and applying it to every circumstance and condition of everyday life.

Whether there were specially equipped general *schools* with buildings or rooms set apart for that purpose at this time, cannot be determined from the material available. But that *reading* and *writing* were general, common accomplishments, is evident from several passages. That Shaphan the scribe was also the reader in public cannot be advanced as a valid counter-argument, 2 Kings 22, 8 ff. 2 Kings 23, 2. 2, Chron. 34, 18. The writing of letters by Jehu and the reading of them by the elders of Jezreel is not recorded as anything extraordinary, 2 Kings 10, 1. "Read this (book) I pray thee: and he saith, I cannot for it is sealed: And the book is delivered to him that is not learned, saying, Read this, I pray thee: and he saith, I am not learned," Is. 29, 11, 12. This same example could be used in our days without reproach. It argues *for* a general knowledge of reading, not against it. "Write the vision and make it plain upon tables, that he may run that readeth it," Hab. 2, 2. "Take thee a roll and write therein," Baruch wrote. Jer. 36, 2. Upon the occasion of a transfer of property, Jeremiah subscribed the evidence, but the witnesses also subscribed the book of the purchase, Jer. 32, 10, 12. Both forms of writing were apparently in use, according to these passages: the writing on (clay) tablets and also in rolls.

From all the available material we may conclude that the teaching of the Law, including the prophecies (Torah, Nebiim, Ketubim) was general during the period, that reading and writing was a common accomplishment, and that a great majority of the people, who enjoyed the services of interpreters, scribes, or teachers, also had some knowledge of arithmetic, geography, music, astronomy, arts and crafts. Is. 44, 12, 13. Is. 46, 6.

Before continuing in the discussion of the next period of Jewish history, it must be noted that with the leading away of the Jews into exile, there begins that period of their history which produced the Talmud (in the general, more comprehensive meaning). As soon as Nebuchadnezzer had taken down large numbers of the population of Judea into Babylonia, so tradition has it, king Jehoiachin founded an academy of Jewish learning at Nehardea, erecting a special building for that purpose. This school apparently existed for several centuries. The academy of Ezra was near Huzal. While the Great Synagogue cannot be established as historical, yet there are sufficient evidences of oral tradition leading back to some such body, and making the beginnings of Talmudic interpretation very probable for the period of the exile. It is quite true that there are no authentic written documents, and yet the tradition cannot be ignored.

In order to avoid confusion and to retain the division of historical periods in our discussion, we shall continue to give a short historical survey of the remaining periods of the Jewish history: the Exilic, the Persian, the Hellenic, the Maccabean, and the Roman periods, together with a brief presentation of the status of education from Biblical and Apocryphal sources, and then finally embrace the time from the beginning of the exile to the decline of the academies in Palestine and Babylonia, and discuss the education of this entire period as shown in passages of the Talmud.

III

THE EXILIC PERIOD, 586-536 B. C.

Historical Survey

JERUSALEM and the temple had been destroyed by the Bablyonian invaders. This fact also had a very definite influence on the hopes of the Jews as to their speedy return. Most of them followed the advice of Jeremiah (29, 5-7) and Ezechiel (39) and prepared for a stay of several generations. They built themselves houses and dwelt in them, they planted gardens and ate of their fruit. They were in general, several disagreeable incidents excepted, permitted the free exercise of their religion. They gave up none of their established customs. And since they looked upon the exile as a punishment of God for their laxity and denial, they were more than ever anxious to return to the worship of the true God and the keeping of all the commandments and statutes delivered to Moses. Everything was auspicious, not only for a revival of the revealed religion, but also for quiet internal growth and an almost imperceptible process of assimilation of secular knowledge and learning. From fifty to seventy years they had been in exile, when the promised deliverance came. It was in the year 538 B. C. that Cyrus vanquished the Babylonian army. He made Kyaxares, called by Daniel Darius of Medea, nominal ruler of the empire. But when Darius had died, in 536, Cyrus himself took up the reign. One of his first official acts was a proclamation permitting the exiled Jews to return to their country, not, indeed, as a politically independent people, but with the assurance of full religious liberty. It must be noted, however, that not all the Jews returned to Jerusalem at this time, but only a small part. The younger generation apparently looked upon Babylonia as their home country. But the academies fostered the feeling of nationalism and nourished the hope of the return of the ancient glory.

Education during the Exilic Period

The passages of the Bible concerning the status of education during this period are few in number and very meagre as to contents. But from the material at hand and from the spirit of the writings transmitted to us there can be no doubt that the *same principles* as to the *bringing up* and the education of children prevailed at this time as in the previous periods. Children were esteemed very highly as special blessings of God. One of the most terrible curses pronounced upon the idolatrous Jews was: "Famine and evil beasts shall bereave thee," Ezek. 5, 17. According to this passage, the relation between parents and children was that of kindness and tender solicitude, and to be deprived of children was considered a most terrible visitation of God. The power of parents over their children was practically unlimited, with the object, however, of serving their interests, Jer. 29, 6. On the other hand, a "criminal son shall surely die, his blood shall be upon him," Ezek. 18, 13.

That *systematic instruction* was given, at least in certain circles, seems to be evident from the story of Daniel and his friends. Ashpenaz was told to select from among the captive young men "children in whom was no blemish, but well favored, and skillful in all wisdom, and cunning in knowledge, and understanding science, and such as had ability in them to stand in the king's palace, and whom they might teach the learning . . . of the Chaldeans," Dan. 1, 4, 17. Now although these four were "of the king's seed, and of the princes," yet the text does not in any way limit the accomplishments mentioned to these young men. It seems more in conformity with the words to believe that a fair degree

of knowledge was general among the Jewish young
men, and that these four, in a competitive examination, ranked highest. So far as Daniel is concerned,
Josephus even states that he was "already sufficiently
skilled in wisdom" to meet all the requirements of
the king. Outside of this one passage, special subjects of instruction or study are not mentioned in the
books pertaining to this period. We have no reason
to assume, however, that the ability to read and write
was not a fairly general accomplishment, as well as
the other branches necessary for commercial pur-
suits and professional life. Even the art of map
drawing with the incidental knowledge of geography
and arithmetic, is introduced in a rather casual
manner, Ezek. 4, 1.

There were specially appointed *teachers* during
this period, not primarily, indeed, for secular, but
for religious instruction. Since, however, the inter-
pretative method of teaching made necessary at
least an elementary knowledge of the common school
branches, we may well speak of regular and general
instruction and training, not very elaborate under
the circumstances, to be sure, but still of considerable importance. "They that understand among
the people shall instruct many," Dan. 11, 33. "And
they that be wise shall shine as the brightness of the
firmament; and they that turn many to righteousness as the stars for ever and ever," Dan. 12, 3.

These passages refer to teachers, to them that instruct, to the wise men, and that there were quite a number of them, even during the exile, appears from this very general remark.

IV

THE PERSIAN PERIOD, 538-332 B. C.

Brief Historical Survey

WITH the overthrow of the Babylonian empire, the Jews did not, indeed, regain their liberty, neither in a political nor a commercial respect, but their condition was, nevertheless, ameliorated to a great extent. Cyrus proved rather friendly to them, especially so far as their religion was concerned. Immediately upon his accession to the throne, he issued the proclamation permitting the Jews to return to their country. At the same time, he brought forth the vessels of the house of the Lord, which Nebuchadnezzar had taken as trophies of war from Jerusalem. Under the leadership of prince Zerubbabel and the high priest Jeshua some 60,000 people made the journey back to the desolate city Jerusalem. The first attempts at restoration, especially the rebuilding of the temple, were such pitiful efforts in comparison with the former glory that the older members of the people that had seen Solomon's temple, burst into tears. In addition to that, the Samaritans did everything in their power to hinder

47

the progress of the work. It was not until 516 B. C. that the Jews were able to dedicate their new temple. This was during the reign of Darius Hystaspis.

During the next sixty years, the Jews that remained in Babylonia suffered somewhat from oppression, but were finally liberated in a most glorious manner. Xerxes is very probably the king of whom the Book of Esther speaks. In 458 B. C. the priest and scribe Ezra, who seems to have had some influence at the Persian court, went back to his native country. He had been in charge of an academy in Babylonia and his purpose was to effect a thoroughgoing reform of religion in Judea. A great number of exiles accompanied him and aided very greatly in the work that he had set himself to do. While he had some success, the material prosperity of the Jews at Jerusalem was not enhanced. When Nehemiah, the cupbearer of the Persian king Artaxerxes (Longimanus), heard of this, he was moved to give up his important position and hasten to the aid of his brethren. It was fortunate that the king gave him full commission and power to act, because the state of things at Jerusalem was approaching chaos when Nehemiah appeared. He had the walls repaired and the gates restored. He also, together with Ezra, again established religious services and brought order into the civic body. And when, after his return to his position in the East, the succeeding governors were not equal to the situation, he returned to the city, and eventually drove the Moabite Saneballat, the chief mischief-maker, into Samaria. The next century under Persian sovereignty was comparatively uneventful. During this time of peace, however, the Jews had the best opportunity for readjustment and thorough organization of their educational methods. The influence of the Babylonian academies and the Great Synagogue was being felt with increasing strength. While the extent of this influence cannot be measured exactly, in the absence of authentic information, there can be no doubt that it was very great and lasting.

Education during the Persian Period

All the factors enumerated above: the influence of a strong, but wise government, the reformation of the church and the restoration of the religion of Moses, the contact with people of great enlightenment,—they all had a very definite influence on the Jewish people, especially in education. While secular subjects had never been entirely neglected among them, a new impetus was now given to their study, and the imperative need of a thorough and comprehensive system in education and of a proper equipment for such a system was coming to be felt more and more.

The order regarding the relation between parents and children was obviously insisted upon with greater vigor. The *power of parents* over their children was practically unlimited. The giving and taking in marriage was a right which the parents dared not to abrogate. "Give not your daughters unto their sons, neither take their daughters unto your sons: that ye may be strong and eat the good of the land, and leave it for an inheritance to your children forever," Ezra 9, 12. "Ye shall not give your daughters unto their sons, nor take their daughters unto your sons, nor for yourselves," Nehem. 13, 25. In accordance with this provision of the law, the *obedience of children* and of those under authority was almost absolute. "Esther (as queen) did the commandment of Mordecai, like as when she was brought up with him," Esther 2, 20. Esther had been Mordecai's ward and he had, according to Jewish law, been completely 'in loco parentis' toward her, and she obeyed him as a matter of course. "A son honoreth his father," Mal. 1, 6. That was the self-evident status, the father occupying, by virtue of his parenthood, a position of honor, and the son, by virtue of his sonship, giving his father the respect and obedience due his position.

That *schools* were established in Palestine, at least during the early part of this period, seems very improbable from the material at hand. *Writing* was generally known, and therefore *reading* also, to the Jews in the exile at the time of Xerxes, for the proclamation for the Jews was written in their writing and their language and was therefore evidently read by them also, Esther 8, 9. Whether the bilingual question, with which Nehemiah was obliged to contend at his time, ever reached the schools, is not evident from the passage, Nehem. 13, 24.

Certain it is that *regular teaching* was carried on in the time of Ezra and Nehemiah, but whether this included religious instruction only, or was extended to embrace secular subjects also, does not appear from Biblical sources. The Levites were the regular teachers of the peoples, Nehem. 8, 7, 9. "Ezra had prepared his heart to teach in Israel statutes and judgments," Ezra 7, 10. The "men of understanding" mentioned by Ezra were the teachers of the people, who gave them understanding of the law, Ezra 8, 16, 18. "The priest's lips should keep knowledge," Mal. 2, 7.

The passages adduced here have reference exclusively to religious teaching, or the reading and teaching of the Law. But, aside from evidence which will be introduced later, it would be a mistake to argue 'e silentio' that instruction in secular branches was unknown during this period. It is expressly stated that the teachers not only read the law (taught by rote), but they also "gave the sense and caused the people to understand the reading," Nehem. 8, 8. According to Jewish custom, that can mean but one thing, that they took up all the questions touched upon in the holy books, and heard discussions of the elements of all branches of knowledge.

V

THE HELLENIC PERIOD, 332-165 B. C.

From the Conquest of Judea by Alexander
the Great to the Defeat of the Syrians
by Judas Maccabeus

Historical Survey

THE transition from Persian to Hellenic sovereignty in Judea was attended with but little disturbance, as Josephus relates the story. After the Samaritan leader had renounced allegiance to Darius, and Alexander, after taking the city of Tyre, was marching down through Judea on his way to Egypt, the high-priest Jaddua conceived of a daring plan to gain the good-will of the conqueror. Clad in all his robes of office, attended by the priests, and followed by the inhabitants of Jerusalem, he went out to meet Alexander. His plan succeeded splendidly. Alexander bowed down before Jaddua and explained to his officers that he had once in a dream seen a man in such vestments, who had promised him the conquest of Asia. He then inspected the city and the temple, made a sacrifice on the main altar, excused the Jews from the

53

payment of taxes for one year, and granted them free exercise of their religion. With the death of Alexander, however, only ten years later, the Jewish hopes received a temporary setback. Ptolemaeus Lagus, after a long struggle, gained the mastery over Egypt and Judea. He, as well as his successor, Ptolemaeus Philadelphus, took an active interest in the arts and sciences, and many Jews were induced to move to Egypt with the prospect of great material advantages. Most of these settled at Alexandria, where they became acquainted with Greek learning. The immense library of Alexandria was begun by Ptolemaeus Philadelphus and the translation of the Old Testament into Greek, the so-called Septuagint, was probably made at his instigation.

About the year 247 B. C., the old struggle between the Ptolemies of Egypt and the Seleucidae of Syria was renewed and continued for almost fifty years. Judea was often the battle-ground, and Jerusalem very often had to bear the brunt of the conflict. Antiochus III finally vanquished the Ptolemies and Judea apparently was to have an era of peace and prosperity. Antiochus proved a friend of the Jews, he permitted them to repair the temple, granted full religious liberty, and persuaded many of the Jews to form colonies in various parts of Asia Minor, as well as in Mesopotamia. This happy condition was radically changed under Antiochus the Noble. When one of his favorites, Jason, who had usurped the position of high priest in Jerusalem, and introduced pagan ceremonies, was driven from the city, he began a series of atrocious assaults. Jerusalem was taken, thousands were killed, other thousands sold as slaves, the walls of the city were razed and the Jewish religion was declared obsolete. The final result was that a staunch Jewish patriarch, Mathathias, gathered the faithful about him, entrenched himself in the mountains, made sudden attacks upon the enemy, and gradually recovered a considerable portion of the country. And his son, Judas Maccabeus, took up the work where he had relinquished it. He routed the Syrians in several great battles, took the city of Jerusalem, and restored the Jewish religion.

Education during the Hellenic Period

It appears from the history of this period that there were two eras of quiet, one of rather short duration, at the end of the fourth century B. C., and the other during the time of the first Ptolemies. These periods, especially the latter, were very favorable to the development of the arts and sciences. With Greek learning, especially to the extent in which it was introduced, came, in some measure at least, the Greek system of education. If there was no definite educational or school system established, by which the results of Greek learning were communicated to the young, there must, at least, have been sufficient intercourse to permit of an absorption of Greek learning by the leaders of the Jewish people.   More definite conclusions can be drawn only for the succeeding historical periods, and in the final summary of the entire Talmudic period the additional information will enable us to reach more definite conclusions.

The only book from which we may obtain reliable information, though rather meagre, as to the status of education during this period, is the Book Ecclesiasticus, commonly known as the "Wisdom of Jesus, the Son of Sirach."   The date of this book is given as pertaining to the next period, but its contents belong to this period, since the proverbs were gathered by the men of one family during the course of three generations.   We have, therefore, a fair picture of the conditions and of the ideals of the time, about the end of the third and the beginning of the second century before Christ.

It appears from this book that the educational ideals of earlier times were insisted upon with even greater emphasis at this time.   The new feeling of nationalism and the thorough reformation of the church insisted upon a slavish return to ancient laws and customs, and the movement was aided by the academies and synagogues in the various larger cities and influential centres to such a degree, that literal interpretations of the law and slavish adherence to its very letter was practiced among the conservative Jews, who were the leaders of the people. The *position of the parents* is defined with unequivocal definiteness. "If thou hast children, bring them up well, and bend their neck from their youth up. If thou have daughters, preserve their body and do not pamper them. Counsel thy daughter, then hast thou done a great deed, and give her to a sensible man," Sir. 7, 25-27. "Rejoice not, because thou hast many evil children, neither boast, because thou hast many children, if they fear not God. It is better to have one pious child than a thousand impious. And it is better to die without children than to have godless ones," Sir. 6, 1.3.4. Children were most desirable treasures then, and considered great gifts of God, and their bringing up, their moral training was entrusted to the parents, upon whom the full responsibility rested. The power of the parents was just as unlimited as in any of the previous periods.

On the other hand, the *relation of children to parents* was defined just as exactly. "The Lord will have the father honored of the children, and whatsoever a mother commands the children, He wants the same kept," Sir. 3, 3, 7, ff. "Whosoever honors his father, will live all the longer, and whosoever is obedient for the Lord's sake, is a consolation to his mother"; vs. 9: "Honor thy father and thy mother with deeds, words, and patience, that their blessings may come upon thee. For the blessing of the father builds houses for children, but the curse of the mother destroys them." "Honor thy father with all thy heart, and forget not what a care thou hast been to thy mother," Sir. 7, 29. "An impertinent son is a dishonor to his father. A sensible daughter will very likely get a husband, but a spoiled daughter is unsought and brings care to her father," Sir. 22, 3, 4. "Forget not the teaching of thy father and thy mother, so shalt thou sit among the lords," Sir. 23, 18. Respect, honor, obedience, a careful regard for the teaching of the parents were required absolutely of children, while impertinence, lack of respect, want of shame, and vileness were condemned.

These demands, moreover, were required to be enforced with the utmost strictness. As the home was considered the foundation of the nation and the children the future representatives of God's chosen people before the world, laxity in *discipline* was considered not merely foolish, but almost criminal. Several chapters are devoted almost exclusively to this topic, notably chapters 26 and 30. Some of the significant verses are the following. "If thy daughter be not chaste, keep her very strictly, lest she perform her wantonness, if she have too much liberty," Sir. 26, 13. "He that loves his child, holds it under the rod, in order that he may afterward experience joy from the same. . . . A spoiled child becomes wanton, like a wild horse. . . . Do not give him license in his youth, and excuse not his foolishness," Sir. 30, 1 ff. It may be worthy of note here that the death penalty for an unruly child is not mentioned, but that in general the severity of dealing with a disobedient son is emphasized even more than in previous periods.

So far as *systematic instruction* is concerned, there is no evidence of a general school system at this time, with the exception of religious schools, Sirach 38, 25. 39, 1-15, which were probably conducted, especially in the Diaspora, in connection with the synagogues. But we may infer that the influence of the great academies was far-reaching even at this time and that Greek learning and education was also a factor in determining thought and trend among the leaders of the Jews. Men like Jesus Sirach, for instance, undoubtedly were educated fully up to the demand of the times. It might be argued from Sir. 38, 38, 39, that even such simple accomplishments as reading and writing were unusual at that time. But from that passage as well as from vs. 38 ff. in the next chapter one may argue with equal plausibility that the Book of Ecclesiasticus was written for the use of the general public and that everybody was expected to be able to read its precepts readily. If there is at all such a thing as advancement and building up on an excellent foundation, it would be far more in keeping with the circumstances to infer the existence of religious schools, where elementary training was given, at least in the principal cities. For that these schools did not confine themselves to the teaching of religious and moral precepts, has been emphasized above, and shall be discussed in a more extended manner from the Talmud.

VI

THE MACCABEAN PERIOD, 165-63 B. C.

From the Defeat of the Syrians by Judas
Maccabeus to the Conquest of Jerusalem by Pompey

Historical Summary

AFTER the defeat of the Syrians and the conquest of Jerusalem by Judas Maccabeus, the power of the Syrians was almost broken. The first concession the victorious Jews insisted upon was full religious liberty with all attendant privileges. Jonathan Maccabeus, by a fine stroke of diplomacy, succeeded in obtaining the office of high priest for himself. The third brother, Simon Maccabeus, went a step farther and gained for his family the hereditary ethnarchy. His grandson, Aristobulus, the son of Hyrcanus, changed the government to a kingdom, assuming the title of king for himself. And his brother, Alexander Jannœus practically restored the independence of the kingdom, regaining for it also the extent and virtually the power of the time of David. Owing to the fact, however, that the office

61 """

of king and that of high priest were vested in one person, the more zealous among the Jews incited the people and precipitated a civil war which, a few years later, gave the Roman general Pompey a welcome excuse for intervention. The inevitable result was the conquest of Judea and the seizure of Jerusalem by the Romans, 63 B. C. Aristobulus the king and his children were taken to Rome to be exhibited in the triumphal pageant, and the independence of Judea was a thing of the past.

Education during the Maccabean Period

"At this time there were three sects among the Jews," relates Josephus, "the Pharisees, the Sadducees, and the Essenes," Antiq., Book XIII, Ch. V. This remark is significant, because it shows a high development of learning among the Jews at that time. The era was certainly an auspicious one for advance along all lines, including educational matters. There was, especially at the time of the great festivals, intercourse with the Jews who had founded colonies in Babylonia, in Egypt, throughout Asia Minor, and elsewhere, but retained the religion and all their customs. Ever ready to accommodate themselves to their own advantage, the Jews absorbed the learning of the most civilized nations of the time by contact, if not by actual study in the

foremost schools and universities of the world.   In
one respect alone they remained perfectly isolated,
in their religion and, to some extent, in their language, the Hebrew-Aramaic, which was their home
tongue.   Just how much the Jews advanced along
all lines at this time, will be shown in the discussion
of the Talmudic period.   In the apocryphal books,
we have, for this period, the account of the Mac-
cabees, their wars and the political activity, with no
special reference to educational matters.   There can
be no doubt, however, from passages like 2 Macc.
7, 28, that the love of parents toward their children and their authority was just as great as in former periods.   Incidentally, it is told that the Hebrew
mother nursed her child about three years, this, then,
being considered the time of infancy.

VII

THE ROMAN PERIOD, 63 B. C.—70 A. D.

Historical Summary

WHEN the Romans, as Josephus relates, had made Jerusalem tributary to their empire, Hyrcanus II remained at first both high priest and ethnarch, with the full power of both offices. It was not long though before Antipater, upon whom Caesar had already bestowed the privilege of the Roman citizenship, succeeded in becoming the procurator of Judea. By this decree of Cæsar the Jews lost the last vestige of political independence and became a dependent principality. Antipater made his son Phasaelus governor of Jerusalem, and Herod, of Galilee. The Roman Anthony later elevated both of them to the rank of tetrarch. Herod the Great assumed the title of king. After his death, the Jewish country was divided among his three sons, Archelaus having the provinces of Idumea, Judea, and Samaria, with the title of ethnarch; Philip the country east of Jordan, with the title tetrarch; and Herod Antipas, Galilee and Peraea, with the title tetrarch. Archelaus (Matth. 2, 22) began his reign with such acts of cruelty and revenge that he was soon banished to Gaul. After that, these provinces were under the jurisdiction of governors (Pontius Pilate, Felix, Festus, etc.), who, in turn, were responsible to the proprætor or proconsul of Syria. Herod Antipas tried to gain the title of King for himself, but was circumvented by his nephew, Herod Agrippa I, through whose machinations he found himself exiled to Gaul. Herod Agrippa I succeeded gradually in having Palestine made a province separate from that of Syria. He was followed by his son, Agrippa II, who held the title of king. It was under his reign that the party of Zealots in Jerusalem became so strong that they stirred up a rebellion against the Romans. The result is well-known. The Roman general Vespasian began the conquest of the province and made the plans for the siege of the city, and his son Titus took Jerusalem. The conquerors knew no mercy. The city was sacked and plundered, razed and burned. The number of captives remaining is given by Josephus as amounting to 97,000. Seventeen thousand young men were sent to Alexandria as slaves, other thousands were kept for the plays in the arena. The Jewish nation ceased to exist. The Jews were dispersed among all nations. That was in the year 70 A. D.

Education During the Roman Period

There is a great deal more to be said for this period than that which is contained in Biblical passages. Nevertheless, the material from which conclusions may be drawn is comprehensive and satisfactory to a greater extent than in the preceding periods. Whether Roman learning ever exerted a great influence on the Jewish people or their educational system, is not evident and is highly improbable. The superscription on the cross was indeed in the Hebrew, the Greek, and the Latin tongue, but it is probable that the Latin was merely for the sake of the soldiers and to emphasize the fact that judgment had been passed under Roman jurisdiction. In the Roman decrees quoted by Josephus, the separation or isolation of the Jews from the people among whom they were living is commented upon, and they were allowed to live and act in all things according to the customs of their forefathers.

It cannot be a matter of surprise then, that, in their comparative isolation, the Jews retained all their laws and customs, and exercised jurisdiction over the members of their nation in all minor matters pertaining to their Law. The *relation of parents to their children,* their authority, their responsibility, and also the love which they owed their offspring, is emphasized in several cases. "Behold thy father and I have sought thee sorrowing," Luke 2, 48. "If ye, then, being evil, know how to give good gifts unto your children," Matth. 7, 11. "The children ought not to lay up for the parents, but the parents for the children," 2 Cor. 12, 14. "Ye fathers, provoke not your children to wrath, but bring them up in the nurture and admonition of the Lord," Eph. 6, 4. The *relation of the children toward their parents* is again one of respect, love, and obedience. "The child grew and waxed strong in spirit, filled with wisdom, and the grace of God was upon Him. . . . He was subject unto them. He increased in wisdom, and in stature, and in favor with God and man," Luke 2, 40, 51, 52. "Honor thy father and mother, which is the first commandment with promise: that it may be well with thee and thou mayest live long on the earth," Eph. 6, 2. In order to maintain the right relation between parents and children, the *discipline* spoken of in the Law was maintained with all the rigor which the Jews were still permitted to use. "God commanded, saying: Honor thy father and mother; and: He that curseth father and mother, let him die the death," Matth. 15, 4. "What son is he whom the father chasteneth not? But if ye be without chastisement, whereof all are partakers, then are ye bastards, and not sons," Hebr. 12, 7, 8.

Parents were held responsible for at least the religious instruction of their children, for the bringing up in the nurture and admonition of the Lord. The instruction, however, was not confined to the home. The *synagogues* (houses of assembly, of prayer, of teaching) that are mentioned throughout the historical books of the New Testament, had their origin at the time of the first kings: "They have burned up all the synagogues of God in the land," Ps. 74, 8. At the time of the Romans, there was a synagogue in every city of any size in Palestine, as well as in many other cities where the Jews were at all numerous. "Jesus went about all Galilee, teaching in their synagogues," Matth. 4, 23. 9, 35. 13, 54. Mark 1, 21, 39. 6, 2. Luke 4, 15. 13, 10. John 18, 20. There was a synagogue at Antioch in Pisidia (Acts 13, 14), Iconium (Acts 14, 1), Thessalonica (Acts 17, 1), Berea (Acts 17, 10), Athens (Acts 17, 17), Corinth (Acts 18, 4), Ephesus (Acts 18, 19); there were several in Damascus (Acts 9, 2, 20), Salamis in Cyprus (Acts 13, 5), Alexandria in Egypt, and Antioch in Syria. These synagogues were not used for services only, consisting of Scripture readings and prayer, but also for lectures and expositions of the Scriptures (Luke 4, 21 ff.) These lectures may sometimes have been held in the adjoining "house of learning," Acts 19, 19. The school of Tyrannus mentioned in this passage was probably a school patterned after the

Greek "Gymnasia." That there were also other schools at this time, appears from several references in the New Testament. "After three days they found him in the temple, sitting in the midst of the doctors, both hearing them and asking them questions," Luke 2, 46. Here we have a school of a special kind, which will be spoken of later. "Paul was brought up in Jerusalem at the feet of Gamaliel, and taught according to the perfect manner of the law of the fathers," Acts 22, 3. Here we have a school of a still different kind, and apparently a very advanced one, for Paul was versed not only in the Law, but also in secular knowledge, and even showed familiarity with Greek poetry. It is evident, then, that the educational system of the Jews was developed quite highly in this period. Just how far the Jews were advanced, will be evident from the discussion of Talmudic times.

THE TALMUDIC PERIOD

The Talmudic period, though considered as beginning after the destruction of Jerusalem and the dissolution of the Jewish nation, may nevertheless be said to extend back to the time of the exile. There are three principal reasons for this statement. In the first place, as noted above, Jewish tradition in regard to the Great Synagogue and the oral transmission of rabbinical exposition cannot be ignored entirely. In the second place, the nucleus of the Mishna in its unwritten form extends back several centuries before Christ. The cessation of prophecy removed a certain restriction upon writing, and the example of Jesus Sirach was undoubtedly imitated oftener than accounts relate. And lastly, many of the institutions referred to in the Talmud date back several centuries, and the discussion thus throws light on conditions that existed long before the actual gathering of the materials in book-form. It is, unfortunately, extremely difficult to fix dates in the discussion with the necessary exactness, but the approximate time may be given according to tradition.

Even at the time of Jesus, the "tradition of the elders" played an important part in some discussions, Matth. 15, 2, 3, and elsewhere. And the schools of Gamaliel, of Hillel and Shammai, where the precepts of tradition were taught (Mishna) were in a flourishing condition even before the fall of Jerusalem. After the destruction of Jerusalem, Rabbi Johanan ben Zakkai, who had gained the favor of Vespasian, asked permission to establish a school of Jewish law, and when this was given, settled at Jabneh, or Jamnia, near Joppa. In this school, to which Jews from all over the world sent their sons, was begun the final development of the form of the tradition or exposition of the Law. Gamaliel the

Younger and Akiba were especially influential teachers. About the end of the second century, Rabbi Juda ben Simon was the leader of this school. He established as authoritative and decisive the Mishna of Akiba, which probably at this time ceased to be oral and was committed to writing. The Jabneh school was transferred to Tiberias, but soon deteriorated. The scholastic center shifted to Babylon in the production of the Gemara or the Talmud proper. The great teacher instrumental in effecting this change was Rabbi Abba Rab, whose school at Babylon soon had 1200 students. His academy was located at Sura, but was often transferred to Pumbedita. Samuel's academy was at Nehardea, a continuation, according to tradition, of the academy founded by king Jehoiachin.

In the fifth century A. D., Rabbi Aschi had the oral explanations, discussions, decisions, etc., based on the Mishna collected in the Babylonian Talmud. About the same time, the teachers in Palestine made a similar collection, which is known as the Jerusalem Talmud. The Mishna, then, is the oral tradition, or the oral common law of the Jews since the time of the exile, and, in part, probably dating back even farther. The Midrash, or commentary in general, embraces every kind of explanation or elucidation of Scripture, including the Mishna, but especially the Gemara, or Talmud proper, and the Tosephta. The

Haggadah is the illustrative and practical, the Halachah the exegetical commentary on the Old Testament. The Halachah collection of Judahha-Nasi (63 tracts) is generally known by that name, while other collections of Halachah are designated as Baraitha. Among these collections were those called Tosephta. Peters says: "Rabbi Judah Hanassi collected all attainable rulings and precedents and published them in what we call the Mishna (1532 years after the giving of the Torah). . . . Many decisions not included (in the Mishna) were collected later under the name of Boraithoth in a work called the Tosephtha, or Addition (Supplement). . . . Yet other Boraithoth are to be found in the Gemara. The Gemara is a comment on the Mishna, just as the Mishna is a comment on the Torah or Law," p. 7-9.

That the education of the Jews about the time of the destruction of Jerusalem was very highly advanced, is evident from such examples as that of Paul (mentioned above), and that of Josephus. The latter says of himself: "I was brought up with my brother, . . . and I made mighty proficiency in the improvements of my learning, and appeared to have both a great memory and understanding. Moreover, when I was a child, and about fourteen years of age, I was commended to all for the love I had to learning; on which account the high priests and principal men of the city came then frequently to me together, in order to know my opinion about the accurate understanding of points of the law" (Life of Flavius Josephus, No. 2). "For those of my own nation freely acknowledge that I far exceed them in the learning belonging to Jews; I have also taken a great deal of pains to obtain the learning of the Greeks, and understand the elements of the Greek language, although I have so long accustomed myself to speak our own tongue that I cannot pronounce Greek with sufficient exactness; for our nation does not encourage those that learn the languages of many nations, and so adorn their discourses with the smoothness of their periods; because they look upon this sort of accomplishment as common, not only to all sorts of free men, but to as many of the servants as please to learn them. But they give him the testimony of being a wise man, who is fully acquainted with our laws, and is able to interpret their meaning; on which account, as there have been many who have done their endeavors with great patience to obtain this learning, there have yet hardly been so many as two or three that have succeeded therein, who were immediately well rewarded for their pains" (Antiq., Book XX, Chap. XI).

Someone may argue that both Paul and Josephus were exceptions, being extraordinary men, even geniuses or at least unusually gifted. But the facts show that they had the opportunity to study and to advance themselves in knowledge, right in the midst of their own people. Moreover, Josephus writes in a very general way: "Our principal care of all is this, to educate our children well, and we think it to be the most necessary business of our whole life, to observe the laws that have been given us, and to keep those rules of piety that have been deliverd down to us" (Against Apion, Book I).

As a matter of fact, while private schools, prophet schools, academies of learning, and synagogues had been in existence for quite a number of centuries, and some of them, at various times, had been in a flourishing condition, it was in the last century of the existence of the Jewish nation that the Jews advanced still farther and founded a school system for all boys, a public school system, maintained at public expense. Simon ben Shetah, who lived in the reign of Alexander Janneus and queen Alexandra (about 106-70 B. C.) ordered the establishment of schools in all the large cities of Palestine. And during the reign of Agrippa II (44-70 A. D.) Joshua ben Gamla extended this order in so far as it now included all cities of Palestine and fixed a minimum age for school boys as from six to seven years, or, according to another account, the completed fifth year.

The educational maxims scattered throughout the

various tracts of the Talmud enable one to gain a very fair estimate of the educational ideals of the Jews. By the saying: "Who is a wise man? He who learns from everybody," Tract Aboth (IX, 82), regular school instruction was by no means excluded. "A city where there are not ten unemployed men who devote all their time to the study of the Law must be considered as a village," Tract Megilla (VIII, 6 ff.). These men were commonly known as scribes and belonged to the teaching force of the city. There was, then, "no excuse for illiteracy, neither poverty nor family," Tract Aboth (IX, 29-30). There was indeed, at one time, a discussion whether instruction ought not to be restricted to the members of the richer, better families, but apparently the argument for a general, unrestricted instruction prevailed. "The school of Shammai maintain that one shall teach only those who are wise, modest, rich, and come from a good family: the school of Hillel, however, hold that one may teach every one, as there were many transgressors in Israel, and after they had become upright men, pious, and righteous, engaged in the study of the Law, they had the good fortune that from them descended men of uprightness, piety, and righteousness," Tract Aboth (IX, 19). Some of the more gifted scholars among the Jews must have attained to a very high degree of learning, for it is said of the Sanhedrin: "Some of its members must be able to speak seventy languages, so an interpreter would not be needed," Tract Sanhedrin (XV, 40). Women were not entirely excluded from all learning. "It is obligatory for women to hear the reading of the Megilla," Tract Megilla (VIII, 7). The Megilla includes the Song of Solomon, Ruth, Lamentations, Ecclesiastes, and Esther. There is no evidence, however, that women were excluded from the general reading and study of the Law, especially since so many of the ordinances concerned them. Some women among the Jews were even highly educated. "Culture in a woman is better than gold," Peters, p. 159. As for the children, though they were prized very highly, as will be shown presently, their position was always a subordinate one." "One adduces no proof from a minor," Tract Megilla (VIII, 54).

The office of the *teacher* was a highly respected and a most important one. A good teacher was valued as highly as the most important official of the state, though, at times, especially in the academies, he served without pay, Tract Aboth (IX, 35). "The teachers are the guardians of the State," Peters, p. 161. "He who instructs a child is as if he had created it," ibid. "You should revere the teacher even more than the father. The latter only brought you into the world, the former indicates the way into the next. But blessed is the son who has learned from his father: he shall revere him both as his father and his master; and blessed is the father who has instructed his son," Peters, p. 165. This reverence was carried so far that we read: "He who learns from another one chapter, one halachah, one verse, or one word or even a single letter, is bound to respect him," Tract Aboth, Chap. 6, Mish. 3. The teaching and the studying of the Law were placed above everything else. "The honouring of father and mother, acts of benevolence, hospitality to strangers, visiting the sick, devotion in prayer, promotion of peace between man and man, and study in general (remain intact against the exigencies of the world to come), but the study of the Law outweighs them all," Tract Shabbath (Hershon, 13, 49). "The study of the Law is of greater merit to rescue one from accidental death than building the temple, and greater than honoring father or mother," Tract Megilla (Hershon, 13, 49). This fact, that teachers were held in such high respect, is not even changed by reference to the somewhat obscure passage: "Seven have, in the popular regard, no portion in the world to come: a notary, a school-master, the best of doctors, a judge in his native place, a conjuror, a congregational reader, and a butcher," Tract Aboth d'Rabbi Nathan. This difficult passage is, however, explained to some extent by the following: "The judge should ever regard himself as if he had a sword laid upon his thigh, and Gehenna were yawning near him; the best physicians are destined for hell, the most upright butcher is a partner of Amalek." The underlying idea seems to be that school-masters, like the other professional and trades-people mentioned, are so liable to sin grievously in their calling that there is little hope for them to escape everlasting punishment. A teacher was admonished: "Teach the children of the poor without compensation, and do not favor the children of the rich," Peters, p. 163. Only even-tempered men were permitted in this important station. "No irritable man can be a teacher," Tract Aboth (IX, 60, 61). The older and more experienced the teacher was, the greater was his value to the community. "Whom does he resemble who learns from the young? Him who eats unripe grapes and drinks the wine fresh from the winepress. But whom does he resemble who learns from old men? Him who eats ripe grapes and drinks old wine," Tract Aboth (IX, 87). The ideal teacher is described as follows: "The following fifteen customs are ascribed to the sages: He is pleasant in entering, and so also when leaving; is prudent in his fear for Heaven; versed in wisdom; wise in his ways, has a good conception, a retentive memory, is clear in his answers, questions to the point and answers according to the Law; he learns something new from every chapter taught to him; he is going to the wise, he learns for the purpose of teaching it and performing it," Tract Derech Eretz-Zuta (IX, 23). That a teacher who made a habit of flogging was not retained is shown in the case of a school-master who was removed "because he struck too much the pupils," Tract Maccoth (XVII, 40).

The *relation between teachers and pupils* in general was to be one of respect and consideration for each other. The school-children were regarded as the greatest asset of the nation. "The world depends on its school-children," Peters, p. 158. "A town which has no school should be abolished," ibid. "Jerusalem was destroyed because the instruction of the young was neglected," p. 159. "The world is only saved by the breath of the school-children," ibid. "Even for the re-building of the Temple the instruction of the children must not be interrupted," ibid. A great teacher said of himself: "I learn much from my masters, more however from my colleagues, and still more from my disciples," Tract Maccoth (XVII, 25). On the other hand, respectful consideration should actuate the pupil. "If the master err, the scholar should inform him, and not wait until it is published in order to gain honor for himself," Tract Shebuoth (XVII, 50).

So far as *pupils,* disciples, or scholars in general are concerned, there are some interesting classifications to be found in the Talmud. "There are four kinds of pupils: one understands readily but forgets soon—there the advantage is swallowed by the failing; another grasps but slowly and seldom forgets—there the failing is outweighed by the talent; a third understands readily and is slow to forget—his is a good portion; a fourth understands slowly and forgets quickly—his is a poor endowment," Tract Aboth (IX, 131). Almost of the same kind is a passage following shortly after: "There are four kinds of the disciples of the wise: sponge, funnel, strainer, and sieve: sponge—sucking up all things; funnel—allowing all that is received in the one end to flow out at the other; strainer—letting the wine run through and retaining the dregs; sieve—blowing off the bran and keeping the flour," Tract Aboth (IX, 138). A passage which presents the same idea is found a few pages before (IX, 98). That the advantage of absorbing readily, of a perceptive memory, lies with the young, is expressed in the following passage: "One who is taught when young absorbs the words of the Torah in his blood, and he can utter them explicitly, but the reverse is with one who is taught when old. There is also a proverb to this effect: If thou hast not desired them in thy youth, how wilt thou reach them in thy old age?" Tract Aboth (IX, 88, also 85). "To what may he be compared who teaches a child? To one who writes on clean paper; and to what may he be compared who teaches an old man? To one who writes on blotted paper," Peters, p. 162. For a complete religious education a knowledge not only of Scripture, but of the Mishna and Gemara (Midrash) also, including the Halachah, was required. "Whosoever is versed in Midrash, but not in Halachah, has not tasted of wisdom; and he who is the opposite, has not tasted of the fear of sin. . . . One who is versed in Midrash, but not in Halachoth, is like unto a strong man, but who is unarmed; one who is opposite is like an armed weakling. One, however, who is versed in both is like unto a man who is both strong and armed," Tract Aboth (IX, 101). The meaning is that theoretical knowledge and practical application must go hand in hand. The age, at which the various parts of religious instruction should be given, is stated as follows: "One five years old should study Scripture; ten years—Mishna; thirteen years old should practice the commandments; fifteen years old should study Gemara; at twenty, pursue the study of the Law," Tract Aboth (IX, 133). The ages given in this outline are approximately the ages of the pupils in the various schools: infant school, elementary school, secondary school, academy or college.

In *study*, the greatest industry, the most painstaking application was required on the part of the pupil, and, at the same time, the most indefatigable patience on the part of the teacher. "Every disciple who has studied and then abandons his studies, has no share in the world to come. . . . Whoever does not visit the college which is in his city, has no share in the world to come." Tract Aboth (IX, 122). "If you interrupt your studies for one day, it will take you two to regain what you have lost," Peters, p. 162. The patient teaching and learning by rote was carried so far that "Rabbi Perida had a pupil to whom he had to rehearse a lesson four hundred times before the latter comprehended it," and in one case, when the mind of the pupil had been distracted, "he repeated the lesson a second four hundred times," Tract Eiruvin (Hershon, 242, 57). The rule was : "A master is bound to rehearse a lesson to his pupil four times," Tract Eiruvin, Hershon, 73, 26. The rehearsing and the memorizing of a lesson was to be carried on aloud. "It is recorded that Rabbi Eliezer had a disciple who also studied in silence, but that after three years he forgot all that he had learned," Tract Eiruvin, Hershon 224, 29. "Rav says a man should never absent himself from the lecture-hall, not even for one hour; for the above Mishna had been taught at college for many years, but the reason of it had never been made plain till the hour when Rabbi Chanina ben Akavia came and explained it," Tract Shabbath, Hershon, 9, 31. The amount of study expected from a boy was so great that it endangered his health. "A boy at thirteen years of age is bound to observe the usual fasts in full, i. e. throughout the whole day. A girl is bound to do so when only twelve. Rashi gives this as the reason: A boy is supposed to be weaker than a girl on account of the enervating effect of much study," Tract Kethuboth, Hershon, 162, 27. It was only after the efforts of several years had resulted in total failure that a pupil was discouraged from continuing his studies. "A learner who, after five years, sees no profit in studying, will never see it. Rabbi Yossi says, after three years, as it is written (Daniel 1, 4, 5), 'That they should be taught the literature and the language of the Chaldeans,' so educating them in three years," Tract Chullin, Hershon, 88, 35.

The education of the children began at *home,* and the responsibility of the *parents* for the instruction of the children never ceased until they had reached manhood. In order to make the fulfillment of these obligations possible, it was required of *children* that they *honor and obey* their parents. "Where the children honor their parents, there God dwells, there He is honored," Peters, p. 64. "The honor and reverence due to parents are equal to the honor and reverence due to God," ibid. "Respect your parents as you respect Me, says God," p. 65. "A son must, if necessary, feed and support his parents," ibid. "A child owes his life to three: to God, to his father, and to his mother," ibid. "He who honors his father and mother enjoys the fruit in this life, and stores up a treasure for the future," p. 66. "While the son honors his parents, God holds it as if He were dwelling near the child, and were Himself receiving honor," ibid. "Even if it happens that the son is a teacher, yet if the father is present, the son must rise before him in the presence of all his pupils," ibid. "A child must not contradict his father, and when he names him, he must use a term of respect, such as 'my honored father,'" p. 67. "A child must love and honor his parents while they are living, and must love and respect them after they are dead; and as they loved and honored God, he must love and honor God, and thus make his parents live again in his own good deeds," ibid. "If in after life the son prospers and is richer than his father, he must see that his prosperity is shared by his parents. He must not live in greater luxury than they; he must not allow them to suffer poverty while he enjoys wealth," ibid. In order to show to what extent one is bound to honor his father and mother, Rav Ulla told the story of the Gentile son who would not even wake his father, though he had the promise of great gain, should he do so, Tract Kiddushin, Hershon, 274, 13. The general *duty of the parents* toward their children consisted in this that they were responsible for their bringing up and had to make this their special care. "He who loves his wife as his own self, and he who educates his children in the right way, to him applies the divine promise, 'Thou shalt know that there is peace in thy tent ,' " Peters, p. 62. "The daughter is as the mother was," p. 63. "What the child says out of doors, he has learnt in doors," ibid. "What a child speaks in the street, it has heard either from its father or from its mother," Tract Succah (VII, 92). "It is a woman alone through whom God's blessings are vouchsafed to a house. She teaches the children, speeds the husband to the house of worship and instruction, welcomes him when he returns, keeps the house godly and pure; and God's blessings rest upon all these things," Peters, p. 63. "The daughter's doings have been the mother's acts," p. 64. The responsibility of the father included not only the providing of instruction in schools, but the *teaching of a trade* to his sons. "It is a father's duty, not only to provide for his minor children, but also to take care of their instruction, and to teach his son a trade and whatever is necessary for his future welfare," Peters, p. 64. "He who teaches his son no trade is as if he taught him to steal," p. 86. "He who does not teach his son a handicraft trade neglects his parental duty," ibid. "Beautiful is the intellectual occupation, if combined with some practical work," p. 87.   "It is well to add a trade to your studies, you will then be free from sin," ibid.

During the first years of the child's life, from its birth or, more exactly, from the time it was weaned (1 Sam. 1, 24, 2 Macc. 7, 28) till the completed fourth or fifth year, so long as it remained exclusively in the home, the parents had the special duty of beginning its *instruction* in the *Scriptures*.   "As soon as he can talk, his father shall teach him the Torah and to read Shema.   (What is meant by Torah? . . . The verse of Deut. 33, 4: The law which Moses commanded us is the inheritance of the congregation of Jacob.   What is meant by Shema? The first verse, Deut. 6, 4: Hear, O Israel!" The prayer *Kaddish* in its various forms, a liturgical prayer or doxology based upon Ezek. 38, 23, beginning, as a rule, with the words: "Magnified be Thy name, O Lord!" used especially upon very solemn occasions, was also taught in early youth and was thought to have great power, notably also for preserving from Gehenna, Tract Kitzur Sh'eh, Hershon, 332, 10. It is related of Lois, the grandmother, and Eunice, the mother of Timothy, that they instructed him in the Holy Scriptures "from a child," 2 Tim. 1, 5. 3, 15. The expression *apo brephous* shows that the beginning of Timothy's religious instruction had been made in his infancy. That even the very small children were accustomed to religious observances, appears from the following passage: "Children are not made to fast on the Day of Atonement, but when one or two years old, they are accustomed to do it, so that they become habituated to obey the religious commandments," Tract Yomah (VI, 124). In their entire treatment of children parents were warned to be entirely impartial, for nothing so harms discipline as injustice. "A man should never show preference for one child above his other children," Tract Sabbath (1, 19).

With the completion of the fourth or fifth year, according to the order of Joshua ben Gamla, the time came for the pupil to go to the first school, the *infant school,* the Talmudic timukot shel bet rabban, the 'babies of the teacher's house.' This school was later, together with the elementary school, called Heder. It is concerning the discipline in a school of this kind, probably, that we read: "Never tease a young pupil . . . their kingdom is behind their tears (i. e. when they become older they seek revenge)," Tract Pesachim (V, 38). It has been thought that *scribes* had charge of the infant school. Information on the subject is wanting. In the later Heder, a lower Rabbi was teacher. Besides continuing their Scriptural studies (principally by rote), the young pupils were now taught the Hebrew alphabet. A very ingenious and interesting method of making the memorizing of the letters easy, by comparing them with animals and other well-known objects, is given in Tract Sabbath (11, 208). The pupils also learned to count, which was quite easily taught, since the letters of the Hebrew alphabet are, at the same time, their numbers.

With his entry into the *elementary school,* the Bet-ha-Sefer or 'House of the Book,' the boy was fully launched into his education. Boys from their sixth to their completed ninth year attended this school. It happened, however, especially in later years, that children up to the age of thirteen were enrolled in the primary school. It seems that a fee was required of the boys, at least at some time: "To begin the study of the Torah required 200 zuz," Tract Baba Bathra (XIV, 323). If there was no *building* erected for the purpose, a dwelling was converted into a *school-house,* and the equipment was very meagre. There was an elevated place or platform for the teacher. The pupils, in early times, squatted before him on the floor or ground. Later on, at least in some of the schools (Hillel's), there were chairs for the pupils. "Let thy house be the meeting-place of the wise; sit gladly at their feet, and drink in their words with avidity. The house should be for the use of the scholars and their disciples. (The pupil) shall not sit before thee on the bed, chair, or bench, but on the floor, and every word that thou utterest he shall receive with awe, terror, fear, and trembling," Tract Aboth (IX, 27 ff.). Twenty-five children was the highest number of pupils permitted to each teacher in a class for elementary instruction. There should be an assistant appointed, if there be forty in number; and if fifty there should be two competent teachers, Tract Baba Bathra, Hershon, 179, 77. There is a story told in this connection about a teacher's negligence and superficiality which is very significant. The *rabbi* or *city penman,* who taught the boys, was designated as teacher. His Hebrew name was modeled after the Greek *paidagogos.* There were also artisan masters for the instruction in the trades, upon which the Talmud insisted, Tract Sabbath (1, 22). The *religious subjects* taken up in the Bet-ha-Sefer were the book of Leviticus, followed by all the books of the Bible. This is the order in which Aquiba and his son studied. In addition, there was the review of the alphabet and the alphabet backwards, reading and writing, grammar and composition. Some attention was also given to hygiene in the question of proper diet for school-boys, Tract Sabbath, 11, 318. The age of the boys in this school was considered the best for memory work. "He who learns as a lad, what is he like? To ink written on fresh paper. And he who learns when old, what is he like? To ink written on blotted paper," Tract Aboth (IX, 67).

The *secondary school,* Bet-ha-Midrash, the 'house

of study' or 'house of learning,' was the next step in the boy's education. According to rabbinical tradition, this school looks back upon a long term of service. The school of Samuel at Rama (1 Sam. 19, 19) was said to have been one of this type. Solomon built many, Hezekiah fostered them, the young men of the tribe of Issachar, with the aid of Zebulun, the merchant, attended them. At the time of Vespasian, Jewish writers assert, there were 480 schools, Bet-ha-Sefer together with Bet-ha-Midrash, in Jerusalem. There were houses or rooms set apart for the purpose of teaching, called houses of learning, where the pupils sat before their masters, at the time of Hillel, on chairs, Tract Aboth (IX, 137). The average age of the pupils in this school was from ten to fourteen years. The *rabbis*, who had charge of the schools, were not to receive pay from the pupils, Tract Derech Eretz-Zuta (IX, 24). There was evidently a privilege as to choice of teachers, though the passage may refer to academies only. "When thou hast studied under one master, say not: 'It is enough!' but go and study under another. . . . It is a duty to study under three masters. . . . Because thou canst not know which master's teaching will remain with thee, or perhaps all are good," Tract Aboth (IX, 20). The instruction consisted principally in the Mishna, Tract Kethuboth, Hershon, 138, 19, which was memorized and explained because a boy of thirteen was to perform the commandments, Tract Aboth (IX, 133). The reason why there was such a thorough drill in religious instruction with its applications is given: "Without the knowledge of religion there can be no true culture, and without true culture there is no knowledge of religion. Where there is no wisdom, there is no fear of God, and without fear of God there is no wisdom," Tract Aboth (IX, 79). There was special zeal in the effort to get the lessons soon and not procrastinate. "Children in their rabbi's house (school) have arranged their paragraphs and read before the lamplight," Tract Sabbath (1, 24). The course of study was an unintermittent one. "Why do disciples die while young? Not because they are adulterers, or robbers, but because they interrupt their studies, and occupy themselves with idle conversation, and also because they do not begin again where they stopped," Tract Aboth (IX, 93 ff.). The *discipline* of the school was, according to rabbinical rules, administered with the greatest wisdom. "Mar Zutra the Pious, when a young scholar was delinquent and deserving to be reprimanded, first reprimanded himself and then the young scholar," Tract Moed Katan (VII, 33).

It may be interesting, before continuing in the discussion of the college, to note that there was a similar institution called Bet Waad, 'meeting-place of scholars,' in the days of Jose ben Jaezer of Zereda in Maccabean times, where the hearers or disciples sat on the ground before their teachers.

There was one high school of special renown in Jerusalem in the temple hall, where advanced pupils were admitted and discussions of the Law and the Mishna were held. That was the Bet ha-Midrash-ha-gadol, which the boy Jesus visited, when he was twelve years old, Luke 2.

The *college* was the meeting-place of advanced scholars, such as had finished the Torah and Mishna, as well as the elementary studies in other branches. For though the Jews made religious teaching the basis of all instruction, yet they did not by any means confine their school system to religious instruction. "It is necessary to have a knowledge of the world, beside a knowledge of the Holy Law," Peters, p. 164. And their aim was certainly a splendid one. "The ultimate end of all knowledge and wisdom is man's inner purification and the performance of good and noble deeds," p. 163. Though the various schools were not so sharply defined as to *age* as in our day, the rule was that the pupils of the college were from fifteen to eighteen or twenty years old. There was a college in every larger city, apparently, because the Talmud speaks of them quite casually, Tract Aboth (IX, 122). The term *academy* seems to have been confined to the schools of the great educational centers of Nehardea, Sura, and Pumbedita, in Babylonia, and Jerusalem, Jamnia, and Tiberias, in Palestine. In many of the colleges the students were evidently crowded for room, because it is stated that four and even six men sat to one (square?) ell, Tract Erubin (III, 119). The colleges seem to have been conducted to some extent on the boarding-school plan. "The disciples of the college ate in the inns of the valley and passed the night at the college," Tract Erubin (III, 171). There was a hostelry (inn) started in the neighborhood of the college of Eliezer, Tract Aboth (IX, 30 ff.). In the college, a teacher was not limited to twenty-five pupils as in the elementary grades, because Hillel the First had eighty disciples, Tract Aboth (IX, 54). Moreover, "in the college the most scholarly has preference to age," Tract Baba Bathra (XIV, 236).

As to the *subjects* taught, the religious subjects of course ranked first. The passages praising the study of the Law are almost innumerable. A few of the shorter ones are: "There is no love such as the love of the Torah. The words of the Torah are as difficult to acquire as silken garments," Tract Aboth (IX, 97). "Turn it and turn it again, etc.," Tract Aboth (IX, 133 ff.). "Study Law in old age as well as in youth, in years of famine as well as in years of plenty," Tract Aboth (IX, 20). The subjects taught are enumerated in Tract Succah (VII, 37 f.) as follows: "Bible, Mishna, Gemara, Halak-hoth, Agadoth, observations of the Bible, observations of the scribes, lenient ones and vigorous ones, the analogies of expression, equinoxes, geometries, the language of the angels and the language of the evil spirits, and the language of the trees, the fables, the great things, the heavenly chariots and the small things, the discussion of Abayi and Rabha." It does not occasion surprise therefore that we hear of lectures on profane subjects by a noted teacher, Tract Pesachim (V, 38). And since the Torah was taught and reviewed in the college, not merely by memorizing, but by discussion and argumentation as well, there was a training in logic and rhetoric which was of great value. There must also have been instruction in medicine given, at least to some extent, because physicians are so often spoken of and various remedies discussed. It is true, of course, that a great many remedies were those of superstitition and witchcraft.

The *training* at the college was a very strict one, and a thorough knowledge was insisted upon. "Scholars engaged in studying Law must stop for the reading of Shema, but they need not stop for prayer," Tract Sabbath (I, 20). "Man should not absent himself from the house of learning, even for one hour. Man should never absent himself from the

house of learning, even when at the point of death,"
Tract Sabbath (I, 161). The explanation was thorough, Tract Erubin (III, 126 ff.). "One shall not
willfully sleep till past the hour of reading the
Shema, for by doing so he neglects the Law. . . .
One should not make a practice of talking to his
wife, sons, or daughters, when he is studying at
home, for by doing so he neglects the Torah. .
One should not lounge with idlers in the market,
lest he neglect the Torah," Tract Aboth (IX, 80,
81). "One who walks by the way and learns, and
breaks off his studying and says, How beautiful is
this tree! and, How fine this furrowed field! is en-
dangering his own life," Tract Aboth (IX, 76).
"Never in my life came a man to the house of learning before me, and I never slept in the house of
learning a long or a short time; I never left a man
in the house of learning when I went away," is the
boast of a great rabbi, Tract Succah (VII, 37).

In regard to the *students* and their *abilities,* we
find some keen observations. "There are four kinds
of visitors in the house of learning: he that goes and
does not practice (i. e. he accepts the lessons without any examination or study of them), the reward
of going only remains with him; he that practices
(i. e. he that studies at home) and does not go, the
reward of practice remains with him; he that does
both is pious; he that enrolls among the college vis-

itors, but neither goes not practices, is wicked," Tract Aboth (IX, 131 f.). "Gamaliel the Elder compares disciples to the following four kinds of fish: an unclean, a clean fish, a fish found in the Jordan, and one found in the Ocean. By an unclean fish is meant a disciple of poor intellect, who, notwithstanding his study of Scripture, Mishna, Halakhoth, and Agadoth, still remains poor-minded. By a clean fish is meant a disciple of rich intellect, who studies Scripture, Mishna, Halakhoth, and Agadoth, and develops his mind. By the fish from the Jordan is meant a scholar who has studied all the mentioned subjects, but has not acquired the faculty of answering questions put to him. And by a fish found in the Ocean is meant a scholar who studied all the above subjects and has the ability of answering the questions put to him," Tract Aboth (IX, 138 ff.).

The subjects, then, in which a Jewish boy, could expect instruction, were: A systematic, thorough instruction in Religion, Reading, Writing, Grammar, Rhetoric, Logic; a less systematic, perhaps somewhat insufficient instruction in Philosophy, Geography, History, Geometry, Physiology and Hygiene, Astronomy, Zoology, Botany, Music, Medicine. The order of subjects taught in the twelfth century was as follows: Reading, Writing, Torah, Mishna, Hebrew Grammar, Poetry, Talmud, Philosophy of Religion, Logic, Arithmetic, Geometry, Optics, Astronomy, Music, Mechanics, Medicine, Metaphysics. This list is given only for the sake of comparison.

In conclusion, it seems but fair and just to say that the comparatively high development of the Jewish educational system has done much to give the race the intellectual prominence which it now enjoys.

BIBLIOGRAPHY

The Hexaglot Bible.

Josephus, Wars of the Jews, Antiquities of the Jews, Against Apion.

Rodkinson's Babylonian Talmud.

Hastings Bible Dictionary.

Schaff-Herzog, Encyclopedia of Religious Knowledge.

Jewish Encyclopedia.

Catholic Encyclopedia.

Matthew Henry, Commentary.

Meyer, Commentary; Lange, Commentary.

Peters, Madison C., Wit and Wisdom of the Talmud.

Hershon, A Talmudic Miscellany.

Kent, History of the Jewish People.

Day, Social Life of the Hebrews.

Delitzsch, Jewish Artisan Life in the Time of Jesus.

Leipziger, Education of the Jews.

Schenk, The Sociology of the Bible.

Cheyne, Jewish Religious Life after the Exile.

Kent, Israel's Historical and Biographical Narratives.

Baehr, Symbolik des mosaischen Kultus.

Goodwin, Moses et Aaron seu Civiles et Ecclesiastici Ritus.